READING POWER

19th Century American Inventors

The Inventions of

Amanda Jones

The Vacuum Method of Canning
and Food Preservation

Holly Cefrey

The Rosen Publishing Group's
PowerKids Press™
New York

Published in 2003 by The Rosen Publishing Group, Inc.
29 East 21st Street, New York, NY 10010

First Edition

Book Design: Daniel Hosek

Photo Credits: Cover, pp. 4, 6, 19 Science, Industry, and Business Library, New York Public Library, Astor, Lenox, and Tilden Foundations; p. 5 courtesy of Arcadia Publishing, *Images of America: Town of Aurora 1818–1930*, © 2000 by Donald H. Dayer, Harold L. Utts, and Janet R. Utts; pp. 7, 9 (top), 10–11, 16–17 © Culver Pictures; pp. 8–9 Smithsonian Institution; pp. 13, 14, 15 United States Patent and Trademark Office; p. 18 © Bettmann/Corbis; p. 21 © Patrick Giardino/Corbis

Library of Congress Cataloging-in-Publication Data

Cefrey, Holly.
The inventions of Amanda Jones : the vacuum method of canning and food preservation / Holly Cefrey.
    p. cm. — (19th century American inventors)
Summary: A brief biography of the woman who helped come up with a better way to can fruits and vegetables.
Includes bibliographical references and index.
ISBN 0-8239-6445-0
1. Canning and preserving—Juvenile literature. 2. Jones, Amanda Theodocia, 1835-1914—Juvenile literature. [1. Jones, Amanda Theodocia, 1835-1914. 2. Inventors. 3. Canning and preserving. 4. Women—Biography.] I. Title. II. Series.
TX603 .C385 2003
641.4'2'092—dc21

                                    2002002113
                                    Rev.

Contents

Young Amanda Jones   4

Teaching and Writing   6

Vacuum Canning   8

A Better Oil Burner   16

The Business Owner   18

Glossary   22

Resources   23

Index/Word Count   24

Note   24

Young Amanda Jones

Amanda Theodosia Jones was born in East Bloomfield, New York, on October 19, 1835. She had 12 brothers and sisters. Jones attended public schools and the East Aurora Academy.

Amanda Jones

East Aurora Academy

Teaching and Writing

When Amanda Jones was only fifteen years old, she became a schoolteacher. She also liked to write poetry. She stopped teaching in 1854, after some of her poems were published in a women's magazine.

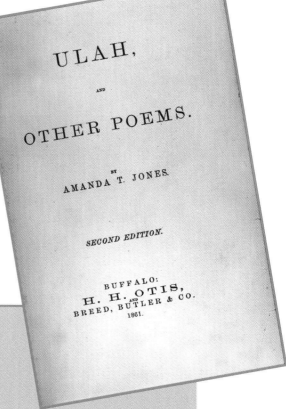

Amanda Jones loved to write. By 1870, she had written two books: Ulah, and Other Poems *and* Atlantis, and Other Poems.

ULAH,

AND

OTHER POEMS.

BY
AMANDA T. JONES.

SECOND EDITION.

BUFFALO:
H. H. OTIS,
AND
BREED, BUTLER & CO.
1861.

In 1869, Jones became an editor of a journal. Then, in 1870, she became the editor of a children's magazine.

Amanda Jones taught in Buffalo, New York, at Buffalo High School.

The Fact Box

In 1859, Amanda Jones was sick with tuberculosis, a very serious lung illness. This illness left her in poor health the rest of her life.

Vacuum Canning

In the late 1800s, preserving food in cans or glass jars and bottles was hard to do. Food had to be cleaned and cooked before it was put into jars or cans. If food was not canned the right way, it could make people sick. Also, most canned foods did not taste good.

Preserving food in tin-coated iron cans was first done around 1810.

Canning companies used advertisements to get people to buy their canned foods.

Around 1872, Amanda Jones thought of a better way to keep the food in cans and jars from rotting. She worked on her idea to preserve food with her cousin, LeRoy C. Cooley.

Years ago, it was common for people to preserve their own food. Some people liked the taste of their own preserved food better than the canned food they could buy in stores. Amanda Jones's food preservation method improved the taste of store-bought canned food.

Jones invented a vacuum method for canning food. Her method would allow fresh, uncooked food to be preserved. Foods preserved by Jones's method were safer to eat and tasted better than foods preserved in other ways.

Apparatus for Preserving Fruit.

No. 139,547.

Patented June 3, 1873.

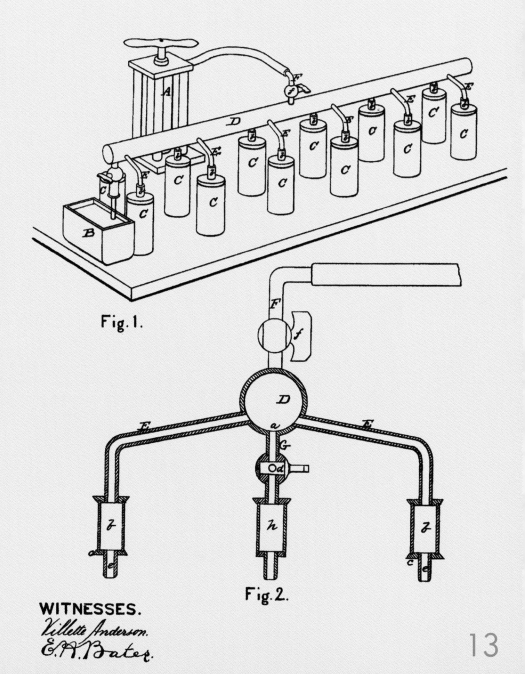

Fig. 1.

Fig. 2.

WITNESSES.

Villette Anderson.
E. A. Bates.

13

Jones's method of canning used fresh, uncooked food. After the food was put into a jar, a tube was used to take the air out of the jar. Then, hot liquid, such as syrup, was put into the jar, and the jar was quickly sealed. Food preserved this way could last a very long time.

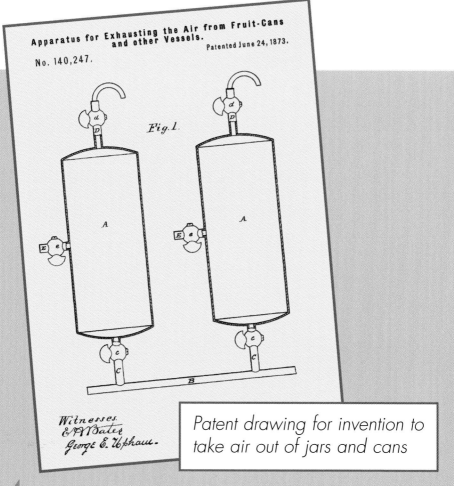

Apparatus for Exhausting the Air from Fruit-Cans and other Vessels.

Patented June 24, 1873.

No. 140,247.

Fig. 1.

A

A

Witnesses.
E.A. Bates
George E. Upham.

Patent drawing for invention to take air out of jars and cans

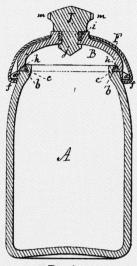

AMANDA T. JONES.

Fruit-Jars.

No. 139,580

Patented June 3, 1873.

Fig.1.

Fig.2.

Fig.3.

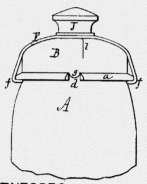

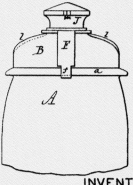

WITNESSES.

Villette Anderson.

Phil C. Masi.

INVENTOR.

Amanda T. Jones,

Chipman Hosmer & Co.

Attys.

Patent drawing for invention of a fruit jar with a special lid to keep food fresh

15

A Better Oil Burner

In 1880, Jones invented a better oil burner. An oil burner is a machine that burns oil to make energy, such as heat. At the time, oil burners were unsafe. Jones made a better oil burner by putting in a safety valve that controlled the amount of oil that could be burned at one time.

Jones got her idea to make a better oil burner after she visited oil fields in northeastern Pennsylvania.

17

The Business Owner

In 1890, Amanda Jones started a company in Chicago to sell canned foods. The company used Jones's vacuum canning method to can puddings and other foods, such as lunch meats and fruit.

Chicago, 1890

All of the workers at Amanda Jones's food preserving company were women.

"This is a woman's industry....This is a business training school for working women."
—Amanda Jones

Amanda Jones died in 1914 in Brooklyn, New York. She was an inventor, writer, and businesswoman. Her vacuum canning method changed the way food was preserved and sold. Today, over 1,500 kinds of food are canned.

Time Line

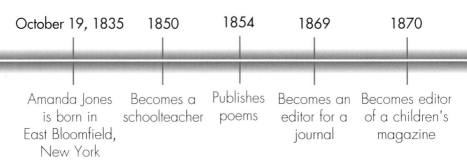

October 19, 1835	1850	1854	1869	1870
Amanda Jones is born in East Bloomfield, New York	Becomes a schoolteacher	Publishes poems	Becomes an editor for a journal	Becomes editor of a children's magazine

The Fact Box

More than 27 billion cans of food are made each year in the United States and Canada.

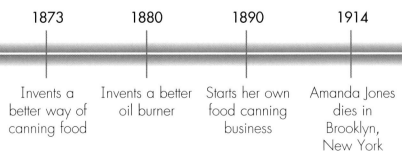

1873	1880	1890	1914
Invents a better way of canning food	Invents a better oil burner	Starts her own food canning business	Amanda Jones dies in Brooklyn, New York

Glossary

academy (uh-**kad**-uh-mee) a private middle school, junior high, or high school

advertisements (ad-vuhr-**tyz**-muhnts) paid notices that companies use to tell people about their goods or services

editor (**ehd**-uh-tuhr) someone who decides what will be printed in a newspaper, magazine, book, or on a Web site

energy (**ehn**-uhr-jee) power that can be used to produce heat or make machines work

industry (**ihn**-duh-stree) a kind of business that makes a particular product, usually in a factory

patent (**pat**-nt) a legal paper that gives an inventor the right to make or sell his or her invention

preserve (prih-**zerv**) to keep food from going bad

published (**puhb**-lishd) to have printed something and made it available to the public

safety valve (**sayf**-tee **valv**) a movable part on a machine that controls the flow of oil, water, or gas

syrup (**ser**-uhp) a thick, sweet mix of water and sugar

vacuum (**vak**-yoom) a sealed space from which all the air or gas has been removed

Resources

Books

Women Invent: Two Centuries of Discoveries That Have Shaped Our World
by Susan Casey
Chicago Review Press (1997)

Women Inventors
by Linda Jacobs Altman
Facts on File, Inc. (1997)

Web Sites

Due to the changing nature of Internet links, PowerKids Press has developed an online list of Web sites related to the subjects of this book. This site is updated regularly. Please use this link to access the list:

http://www.powerkidslinks.com/ncai/iaj/

Index

A
academy, 4–5

B
businesswoman, 20

C
canned food, 8–9, 11, 18
Cooley, LeRoy C., 10

E
editor, 7, 20
energy, 16

S
safety valve, 16
schoolteacher, 6, 20
syrup, 14

Word Count: 425

Note to Librarians, Teachers, and Parents

If reading is a challenge, Reading Power is a solution! Reading Power is perfect for readers who want high-interest subject matter at an accessible reading level. These fact-filled, photo-illustrated books are designed for readers who want straightforward vocabulary, engaging topics, and a manageable reading experience. With clear picture/text correspondence, leveled Reading Power books put the reader in charge. Now readers have the power to get the information they want and the skills they need in a user-friendly format.